PROFILE OF THE PEAKS

Above The down 'Thames—Clyde Express', then coded 1S68, heads north past Wortley Junction, Leeds on 16th August 1966 headed by Holbeck allocated 'Peak' No. D16 (45 016). The 55A shed plate can be seen in the centre of the yellow warning panel.

Gavin Morrison

On 16th July 1977, the 10.03 Newcastle—Liverpool Lime Street climbs the 1 in 105 bank from Huddersfield to Marsden through Paddock Cutting, headed by Gateshead allocated 'Peak' No. 46 047.

Gavin Morrison

PROFILE OF THE PEAKS

BY

J.S. WHITELEY
&
G.W. MORRISON

Oxford Publishing Co.

ISBN 86093 165 X

Typesetting by Aquarius Typesetting Services
New Milton, Hants.

Above   The last Class 46 locomotive, built in January 1963, No. 46 056, prepares to leave Birmingham New Street with the 14.20 to Bristol on 25th August 1980.

Gavin Morrison

Published by:
Oxford Publishing Co.,
Link House,
West Street,
POOLE, Dorset

Photo-reproduction and offset printing plates by Oxford Litho Plates Ltd.

Printed in the City of Oxford by Blackwell (Printing) Limited

Above On 17th May 1980, No. 45 019 is seen shortly after leaving Carlisle with the 11.50 Glasgow Central—Nottingham. Note the unique filled in front, a modification carried out after this engine had been involved in a collision.

John Whiteley

Introduction

Following earlier volumes in the 'Profile' series by OPC covering main line diesel and electric locomotives of Classes 40, 24, 25, 26, 27, 76 and 77 together with 'Deltics' and 'Westerns', we have prepared an album covering the Class 44, 45 and 46 'Peaks', showing them at work on a wide variety of trains throughout the British Rail network, from shortly after their introduction to the present time. We have derived a great deal of pleasure from taking the majority of the pictures of these photogenic locomotives ourselves, and to friends and fellow photographers who have contributed the remainder of the pictures, we offer our grateful thanks, as we do to Janet Blackburn who typed the manuscript.

No. D1 was built at Derby Works for British Rail in co-operation with Sulzer, and on 14th July 1959 it was officially named *Scafell Pike* at a ceremony at Carlisle Citadel station performed by Sir Fergus Graham, Lord Lieutenant of Cumberland. It entered revenue-earning service the following month on 15th August, and was allocated to Camden, although in fact it was on loan to Derby. The other nine members of the class, Nos. D2—D10 entered service between September 1959 and February 1960. They were all named after mountains in the north of England and Wales, and so the class came to be nicknamed 'Peaks', embracing not only the Class 44s, as they were renumbered, but also the later and slightly modified Class 45s and 46s.

During the very early part of their career, Nos. D1—D10 were employed on a variety of duties including St. Pancras—Manchester trains, and then in the spring of 1960 they began work on the LMR Western lines, often handling Euston—Blackpool and Crewe—Perth turns, whilst mainly allocated to Camden.

Later in 1960, during September, No. D8 *Penyghent* worked a series of brake-fitted mineral train trials with a dynamometer car, between Toton and Brent. This signalled what was to prove to be ultimately their lot, and by March 1962 almost the entire class was transferred to Toton for use on freight workings. No. D2 *Helvellyn* was the last member of the class to arrive at Toton, in August 1962 from Crewe North, and there they remained until all were withdrawn from service.

The Class 44s were equipped with a 12 cylinder Sulzer engine of 2,300 h.p. The later and improved Class 45s and 46s, however, were given 2,500 h.p. engines and were slightly heavier at 136 tons and 138 tons respectively, compared to the 133 tons of the Class 44s. These later Class 45s and 46s were soon hard at work on the Midland line and it did not take very long for them to penetrate virtually the whole of the British Rail network on both accelerated freight and passenger services in an extremely successful and efficient manner.

For over twenty years they have been a familiar sight on the most exacting duties over some of the most attractive lines in the country, notably those in Devon and Cornwall, cross country routes from the north of England and the main line from St. Pancras to the Midlands and the north. Until recently, they have been the mainstay of passenger services north from Leeds over our beloved Settle and Carlisle line which now, sadly, no longer carries through trains to Glasgow and is in imminent danger of closure.

Suffice it to say that to this day the 'Peaks' are a welcome sight to both railwayman and enthusiast alike, and long may they remain a familiar part of the modern railway scene.

J. S. Whiteley
Shipley
October 1982

Class 44

Introduced::	**1959 (Built at Derby)**	
Engine:	**Sulzer 12 cyl. 12LDA28A twin bank pressure charged of 2,300 b.h.p. at 750 r.p.m.**	
Max. Tractive Effort:	**50,000 lb at 20% adhesion**	
Weight:	**133 tons**	
Fuel Capacity:	**790 gallons**	

Transmission:	**Electric. Six Crompton Parkinson 305 h.p. axle-hung nose-suspended traction motors**
Driving Wheel Diameter:	**3' 9"**
Route Availability:	**7**
Maximum Speed:	**90 m.p.h.**
Brake Force:	**63 tons**

New Number	Original Number	Name	Date Withdrawn	New Number	Original Number	Name	Date Withdrawn
44 001	(D1)	*Scafell Pike*	10/76	44 006	(D6)	*Whernside*	1/77
44 002	(D2)	*Helvellyn*	4/79	44 007	(D7)	*Ingleborough*	11/80
44 003	(D3)	*Skiddaw*	7/76	44 008	(D8)	*Penyghent*	11/80
44 004	(D4)	*Great Gable*	11/80	44 009	(D9)	*Snowdon*	5/79
44 005	(D5)	*Cross Fell*	4/78	44 010	(D10)	*Tryfan*	5/77

Plate 1 Above   The nameplate bolts still show clearly on No. 44 005 (formerly *Cross Fell*) as it stands in Toton shed yard only one week before being withdrawn from service on 23rd April 1978. No. 44 004, again without nameplates, can be seen at the rear.

Gavin Morrison

Plate 2 Right No. 10 *Tryfan* (44 010) in green livery, stands outside Toton depot in June 1971, shortly after losing the D prefix from its number. No. D4 *Great Gable* was the first of the class to be given unlined blue livery, in February 1967, the last one being No. 44 006 *Whernside* in September 1973, also being the first of the class to be renumbered, officially on 1st October 1973.

B. J. Nicolle

Plate 3 Below No. 44 009 (formerly *Snowdon*) passes Bennerley Junction, Ilkeston on 28th July 1978. This picture shows the indicator panel fitted to one end of the locomotive only, following an accident near Trent. All other Class 44s carried disc type headcodes. T. Boustead

Plate 4 Right No. 44 008 (formerly *Penyghent*) passes Stanton Gate on a Goole—Wolverhampton steel train on 28th September 1979. The locomotive has been specially painted by Toton depot with a white roof and a line along the side. It has also been given a red buffer beam with Toton painted on it. The repainting was done for one of the very popular Toton open days and does a lot to brighton up the normally rather dull livery.

B. J. Nicolle

Plate 5 Above   A Toton-Whitemoor freight near Helpston is seen headed by No. 44 004 (formerly *Great Gable*) on 25th August 1978.

T. Boustead

Plate 6 Below   No. D9 *Snowdon* (44 009) on humble duties working a track recovery train from the Leen Valley line at Bulwell Common. It is heading towards Derby Friargate on 13th July 1969 on the only through track remaining at this time.

T. Boustead

Plate 7 Above An impressive view of No. 44 004 (formerly *Great Gable*) as it heads past Coates Park, near Alfreton, with a Toton to Tinsley freight on 27th June 1979.

T. Boustead

Plate 8 Right All clear for No. 44 007 (formerly *Ingleborough*) as it approaches Barrow Hill, Staveley, with an up steel train from the Sheffield area on 11th September 1979. A tanker train can be seen heading north in the top right hand corner of the picture.

Gavin Morrison

Class 45/0

Class 45/0 locomotives are fitted with steam heating (some isolated)

Introduced:	1960 (Built at Crewe & Derby)	Transmission:	Electric. Six Crompton Parkinson 305 h.p. axle-hung nose-suspended traction motors
Engine:	Sulzer 12 cyl. 12LDA28B twin bank with inter-cooling of 2,500 b.h.p. at 750 r.p.m.		
Max. Tractive Effort:	55,000 lb at 22.1% adhesion	Driving Wheel Diameter:	3′ 9″
Weight:	136 tons	Route Availability:	7
Fuel Capacity:	790 gallons	Maximum Speed:	90 m.p.h.
		Brake Force:	63 tons

New Number	Original Number	New Number	Original Number	New Number	Original Number	New Number	Original Number	New Number	Original Number
45 001	(D13)	45 016	(D16)	45 030	(D31)	45 051	(D74)	45 066	(D114)
45 002	(D29)	45 017	(D23)	45 031	(D36)	45 052	(D75)	45 067	(D115)
45 003	(D133)	45 018	(D15)	45 032	(D38)	45 053	(D76)	45 068	(D118)
45 005	(D79)	45 019	(D33)	45 033	(D39)	45 054	(D95)	45 069	(D121)
45 007	(D119)	45 020	(D26)	45 034	(D42)	45 056	(D91)	45 070	(D122)
45 008	(D90)	45 021	(D25)	45 035	(D44)	45 057	(D93)	45 071	(D125)
45 009	(D37)	45 024	(D17)	45 036	(D45)	45 058	(D97)	45 072	(D127)
45 010	(D112)	45 025	(D19)	45 037	(D46)	45 061	(D101)	45 073	(D129)
45 011	(D12)	45 026	(D21)	45 038	(D48)	45 062	(D103)	45 074	(D131)
45 012	(D108)	45 027	(D24)	45 042	(D57)	45 063	(D104)	45 075	(D132)
45 013	(D20)	45 028	(D27)	45 047	(D69)	45 064	(D105)	45 076	(D134)
45 015	(D14)	45 029	(D30)	45 050	(D72)	45 065	(D110)	45 077	(D136)

New Number	Original Number	Name	New Number	Original Number	Name
45 004	(D77)	Royal Irish Fusilier	45 044	(D63)	Royal Inniskilling Fusilier
45 006	(D89)	Honourable Artillery Company	45 045	(D64)	Coldstream Guardsman
45 014	(D137)	The Cheshire Regiment	45 046	(D68)	Royal Fusilier
45 022	(D60)	Lytham St. Annes	45 048	(D70)	The Royal Marines
45 023	(D54)	The Royal Pioneer Corps	45 049	(D71)	The Staffordshire Regiment
45 039	(D49)	The Manchester Regiment			(The Prince of Wales's)
45 040	(D50)	King's Shropshire Light Infantry	45 055	(D84)	Royal Corps of Transport
45 041	(D53)	Royal Tank Regiment	45 059	(D98)	Royal Engineer
45 043	(D58)	The King's Own Royal Border Regiment	45 060	(D100)	Sherwood Forester

Plate 9 Above   On 27th June 1961, No. D31 (45 030), in original condition, waits to take over a northbound express from Leeds City. This part of the station is now only used for parcels traffic.

Gavin Morrison

Class 45/1

Class 45/1 locomotives are fitted with electric train heating equipment
Max. Tractive Effort: 55,000lb at 22.5% adhesion

New Number	Original Number		New Number	Original Number	Name
45 101	(D96)		45 104	(D59)	The Royal Warwickshire Fusilier
45 102	(D51)		45 111	(D65)	Grenadier Guardsman
45 103	(D116)		45 112	(D61)	Royal Army Ordnance Corps
45 105	(D86)		45 118	(D67)	The Royal Artilleryman
45 106	(D106)		45 123	(D52)	The Lancashire Fusilier
45 107	(D43)		45 135	(D99)	3rd Carabinier
45 108	(D120)		45 137	(D56)	The Bedfordshire and Hertfordshire Regiment (T.A.)
45 109	(D85)		45 143	(D62)	5th Royal Inniskilling Dragoon Guards
45 110	(D73)		45 144	(D55)	Royal Signals
45 113	(D80)				
45 114	(D94)				
45 115	(D81)				
45 116	(D47)				
45 117	(D35)				
45 119	(D34)				
45 120	(D107)				
45 121	(D18)				
45 122	(D11)				
45 124	(D28)				
45 125	(D123)				
45 126	(D32)				
45 127	(D87)				
45 128	(D113)				
45 129	(D111)				
45 130	(D117)				
45 131	(D124)				
45 132	(D22)				
45 133	(D40)				
45 134	(D126)				
45 136	(D88)				
45 138	(D92)				
45 139	(D109)				
45 140	(D102)				
45 141	(D82)				
45 142	(D83)				
45 145	(D128)				
45 146	(D66)				
45 147	(D41)				
45 148	(D130)				
45 149	(D135)				
45 150	(D78)				

Plate 10 Above No. 45 129 leaves Leeds City station on 7th April 1980 with the 10.25 Nottingham—Glasgow.

John Whiteley

Plate 11 Below No. 45 129 stands outside Leeds City station awaiting the arrival of the Nottingham- Glasgow train on 7th April 1980.

John Whiteley

Class 46

Introduced:	**1961 (Built at Derby)**		Transmission:	**Electric. Six Brush axle-hung nose-suspended traction motors**
Engine:	**Sulzer 12 cyl. 12LDA28B twin bank pressure charged with inter-cooling of 2,500 b.h.p. at 750 r.p.m.**		Driving Wheel Diameter:	**3' 9"**
Max. Tractive Effort:	**55,000 lb at 21.8% adhesion**		Route Availability:	**7**
Weight:	**138 tons**		Maximum Speed:	**90 m.p.h.**
Fuel Capacity:	**790 gallons**		Brake Force:	**63 tons**

New Number	Original Number	New Number	Original Number	New Number	Original Number	New Number	Original Number	New Number	Original Number
46 001	(D138)	46 012	(D149)	46 023	(D160)	46 035	(D172)	46 046	(D183)
46 002	(D139)	46 013	(D150)	46 024	(D161)	46 036	(D173)	46 047	(D184)
46 003	(D140)	46 014	(D151)	46 025	(D162)	46 037	(D174)	46 048	(D185)
46 004	(D141)	46 015	(D152)	46 027	(D164)	46 038	(D175)	46 049	(D186)
46 005	(D142)	46 016	(D153)	46 028	(D165)	46 039	(D176)	46 050	(D187)
46 006	(D143)	46 017	(D154)	46 029	(D166)	46 040	(D177)	46 051	(D188)
46 007	(D144)	46 018	(D155)	46 030	(D167)	46 041	(D178)	46 052	(D189)
46 008	(D145)	46 019	(D156)	46 031	(D168)	46 042	(D179)	46 053	(D190)
46 009	(D146)	46 020	(D157)	46 032	(D169)	46 043	(D180)	46 054	(D191)
46 010	(D147)	46 021	(D158)	46 033	(D170)	46 044	(D181)	46 055	(D192)
46 011	(D148)	46 022	(D159)	46 034	(D171)	46 045	(D182)	46 056	(D193)

Named locomotive: 46 026 (D163) Leicestershire and Derbyshire Yeomanry

Plate 12 Above The only named Class 46, No. 46 026 *Leicestershire and Derbyshire Yeomanry*. It is seen at Holbeck, Leeds, in ex-works condition on 18th October 1979.

Gavin Morrison

Plate 13 Left On 1st May 1977, the 15.58 Newcastle—Liverpool express races up the East Coast Main Line near Raskelf behind No. 46 033.

John Whiteley

Plate 14 Above A late arrival at Leeds on the evening of 13th December 1980 is No. 45 001 with the 10.52 terminating train from Paignton.

John Whiteley

Plate 15 Below The interior of the cab of No. 46 010 can be seen in this time exposure taken at York. The locomotive is awaiting departure with the 21.50 mail and passenger to Shrewsbury on 15th September 1980.

John Whiteley

Peaks at Night

Under Repair at Derby

Plate 16 Left A very clean and tidy Derby workshop with work about to start on e.t.h. fitted Class 45, No. 45 145.

John Vaughan

Plate 17 Below With the dents and corrosion holes now filled in, No. 46 048 awaits transfer to the paint shop at Derby.

John Vaughan

Plate 18 Right Minus bogies and nose section, No. 45 011 receives a heavy repair at Derby. All Class 44, 45 and 46 heavy repairs and overhauls were carried out at BREL Derby until early 1982.

John Vaughan

Plate 19 Below A general view of the main repair shop at Derby, showing five 'Peaks' receiving attention.

British Rail

Front End Differences

Plate 20 Left   The first batches of Class 45 'Peaks' were fitted with separate indicator panels. No. 45 025 crosses the Lunds near Garsdale, on 1st March 1980, with the 10.25 Nottingham—Glasgow.
John Whiteley

Plate 21 Below A couple of Class 08 shunters are busy in Hunslet yard, Leeds, on 14th May 1979, as No. 45 133, fitted with a split centre panel, passes under a gantry with the 09.35 Carlisle—Nottingham.

Gavin Morrison

Plate 22 Above The latest filled in front, incorporating two lights, has been fitted to No. 45 046 *Royal Fusilier.* The locomotive is accelerating away from Leeds past Wortley Junction with the 10.25 Nottingham—Glasgow on 27th April 1979.

Gavin Morrison

Plate 23 Below The exhaust from No. 45 019 distorts a factory chimney as it approaches Leeds City station with a short freight. This locomotive is fitted with the undivided centre indicator panel.

Gavin Morrison

Peaks in the Snow

Plate 24 Above   This superb picture of No. 46 042 crossing Byker Bridge, Newcastle, on 18th February 1978 with the empty stock off the 08.10 from Liverpool, captures the wintry conditions encountered in the north-east during the early part of 1978.

P. J. Robinson

Plate 25 Right Even worse weather will be ahead for No. 45 013 in the hill country of the Settle—Carlisle line. It is seen here, passing Guiseley Junction, Shipley, heading the 10.25 Nottingham—Glasgow on 29th January 1979.

John Whiteley

Plate 26 Below A very wintry scene, on 26th February 1977, as the 10.02 Newcastle to Liverpool train is about to enter Standedge Tunnel. The shadow of the signal is seen on the frozen canal.

Gavin Morrison

Plate 27 Above An impressive line up of 'Peaks' and one Class 25, all in green livery, on Holbeck shed, Leeds on 19th February 1963.

John Whiteley

Plate 28 Below Ex-works 'Peak' No. 46 040 is seen at the back of Haymarket shed on 3rd June 1978.

Gavin Morrison

Plates 29 & 30 Above & Right Standing at Toton depot, on 22nd April 1978, is Class 45/0, No. 45 014 *The Cheshire Regiment*. A close up picture of the nameplate, together with the regimental crest, is also shown.

Gavin Morrison

Plate 31 Below A portrayal, in close up, of ex-works No. 46 026 *Leicestershire and Derbyshire Yeomanry* at Holbeck depot, Leeds, on 18th October 1979.

Gavin Morrison

Peaks Around the Regions

Midland

Plate 32 Left   No. 46 009 emerges from the tunnels to the west of Birmingham New Street station with the stock for the 09.25 to Paignton on 11th August 1979.

J. Chalcraft

Scotland

Plate 33 Right   No. 26 (45 020) enters Glasgow Central, on 25th June 1974, with the down 'Thames—Clyde Express'.

D. Cross

Southern

Plate 34 Below   No. 36 (45 031) passes Clapham Junction with a down transfer freight for the Midland Region on 18th September 1974.

B. Morrison

Western

Plate 35 Right A Class 45 heads west out of Taunton under the impressive signal gantry, heading the 09.58 Bradford—Paignton in June 1979.

John Vaughan

Eastern

Plate 36 Below On 18th April 1981, No. 45 009 leaves platform 9 at York with the Saturday 07.52 Newcastle—Poole. However, considerably more attention is being paid to the steam locomotive which can just be seen above the first coach, which had arrived a little earlier with a special from Hull to Chester. On the left of the picture a Class 47 locomotive is just leaving with a Newcastle train.

John Whiteley

Named Peaks

Plate 37 Right Twenty six Class 45 'Peaks' have been named, several of these names having previously been carried by steam locomotives of the 'Royal Scot' and 'Patriot' classes. On Saturday, 3rd February 1979, No. 45 045 *Coldstream Guardsman* is seen near Shipley on the heavy (S.O) 12.30 Bradford Forster Square—Red Bank empty van train.

John Whiteley

Plate 38 Below On 28th July 1975, the up 'Thames—Clyde Express' passes the site of Wakefield motive power depot headed by No. 45 143 *5th Royal Inniskilling Dragoon Guards.* This through service from Glasgow to St. Pancras was discontinued in 1976.

Gavin Morrison

Plate 39 Right No. 45 137 *The Bedfordshire and Hertfordshire Regiment (T.A.)* is overlooked by the high-rise flats of Sheffield as it leaves Midland station with the 15.00 to St. Pancras on 21st April 1979.

John Whiteley

Plate 40 Below No. 45 023 *The Royal Pioneer Corps* heads an up merry-go-round coal train just south of Bridge Junction, Doncaster, on 26th March 1981. Notice how the track has been re-aligned for Inter City 125 services.

Gavin Morrison

On Passenge
Duty in
Cornwall

Plate 41 Left Toton based No. 45 003 emerges from the short tunnel at the east of Redruth station heading the 07.38 Leeds—Penzance on 12th April 1979.

Gavin Morrison

Plate 42 Below No. 46 020 descends into Lostwithiel, also at the head of the 07.38 Leeds—Penzance on the following day, 13th April 1979.

Gavin Morrison

Plate 43 Above   A superb view of No. 46 009, on 21st September 1979, threading its way slowly down the Luxulyan Valley towards Par, at the head of the 10.32 (F.O.) Newquay to Manchester Piccadilly. The photograph is taken from the Treffy Viaduct.

John Vaughan

Plate 44 Left No. 46 020, at the head of a mixed freight train, meanders through Cornwall on the descent from Treverran Tunnel to Par on 19th May 1975.

P. J. Robinson

Plate 45 Below Seagulls fly overhead as No. 46 028 arrives at Par from St. Blazey with some china clay empties on 26th October 1978. The locomotive will run round its train here and then head it west to pick up a load at Burngullow in addition to working a trip up the Drinnick Mill line. A Class 37 and van can be seen heading round to St. Blazey.

Gavin Morrison

On Freight in Cornwall

Plate 46 Above Rumbling along the old single track Fowey branch with a Carne Point clay train is No. 45 063 passing Golant Harbour on 14th June 1978.

John Vaughan

Plate 47 Below No. 46 028 arrives at Burngullow with china clay empties from St. Blazey on 26th October 1978. A Class 08 shunter can be seen in the background.

Gavin Morrison

Plate 48 Above A most impressive view of No. 45 056 on 15th June 1978 making an all out effort whilst climbing Hemerdon bank with a heavy cement train.

John Vaughan

The South Devon Banks

Rattery

Plate 49 Right   A vigorous departure is being made by No. 45 017 as it leaves Totnes and starts the 1 in 66 climb to Rattery box heading a Bristol—Plymouth express on 12th August 1975.

Gavin Morrison

Plate 50 Below   No. 45 053 is storming up to Dainton Tunnel on 4th July 1979 heading the 09.20 Liverpool—Penzance.

B. Morrison

Dainton

Peaks in Devon

Plate 51 Left No. 46 048 rushes through Tiverton Junction heading an express from the Midlands. This once busy junction is showing distinct signs of decay on 5th September 1975.
Gavin Morrison

Plate 52 Below An up mixed freight from Newton Abbot labours up the climb to Whiteball Tunnel behind No. 45 024 on 26th May 1978.

John Vaughan

Plate 53 Above   On 12th August 1975, No. 45 017 passes Aller Junction at the foot of Dainton bank as it nears Newton Abbot heading the 14.01 Plymouth—Leeds train.

Gavin Morrison

Plate 54 Below   On 16th August 1975, No. 45 001 heads north along the seafront between Dawlish and Dawlish Warren. Note that the locomotive was still carrying its number at both ends at this date.

Gavin Morrison

Plate 55 Left   No. 45 076 and No. 45 007 are passing Osmanthorpe near Leeds with an excursion from the north-east on 21st May 1980. No. 45 007 had failed near Garforth and as a result, No. 45 076 had been despatched from Holbeck MPD to rescue the train.

Gavin Morrison

Plate 56 Below   On 10th June 1979, Class 47, No. 47 460, sporting a silver painted roof, piloted Gateshead allocated 'Peak' No. 46 035 past Farnley, Leeds on a permanent way train from Batley. The two locomotives were needed to provide sufficient braking capacity on this unfitted train down the steep incline to Whitehall Junction, Leeds.

Gavin Morrison

Double Headed

Plate 57 Right On 25th June 1978, Class 46, No. 46 036 and Class 31, No. 31 327 pass through the deep cutting at Marsh Lane, Leeds with an eastbound permanent way spoil train.

John Whiteley

Plate 58 Below A most unusual combination in the Leeds Area on 13th March 1980 is seen in the shape of No. 45 038 hauling Class 20, No. 20 180, which is dead but ex-works from St. Rollox, and making its way home to Toton. The train is seen heading south between Holbeck and Hunslet, Leeds.

Gavin Morrison

Peaks Around St. Pancras

Plate 59 Above The graceful 240 ft. span of St. Pancras station dwarfs No. 45 138 as it leaves on the 17.01 to Sheffield, whilst No. 45 115 awaits its next turn of duty on 6th May 1978.

Gavin Morrison

Plate 60 Below On the same day the 13.00 from Sheffield makes a cautious approach to St. Pancras headed by No. 45 150.

Gavin Morrison

Plate 61 Right Gigantic gasometers dominate No. 45 144 *Royal Signals* as it returns light engine to St. Pancras (Cambridge Street) servicing depot on 6th May 1978.

Gavin Morrison

In the London Suburbs

Plate 62 Left No. 45 130, heading an up express, rushes past Kentish Town, which appears deserted, on the Saturday afternoon of 21st May 1977.

Gavin Morrison

Plate 63 Below This once impressive signal gantry shows how the lines at Brent Junction have been rationalized even before electrification, whilst an unidentified Class 45 locomotive hurries past with an up express on 21st May 1977.

John Whiteley

Plate 64 Right No. 45 148, in ex-works condition, passes Hampstead with an up express for St. Pancras on 22nd July 1978.

L. A. Nixon

Plate 65 Below On 21st May 1977, No. 45 131 emerges from the tunnels at Kentish Town on a very light Saturday afternoon parcels train for Bedford.

Gavin Morrison

Plate 66 Above   No. 46 003 of Laira finds itself a long way from home as it leaves the British Steel Corporation's Corby Works with an evening local freight to Kettering and Wellingborough on 21st April 1977.

P. J. Robinson

On the Midland Main Line

Plate 67 Above Rushing past the fine Midland signal box at Glendon North Junction, Kettering, with an up express for St. Pancras on 7th May 1977, is No. 45 136.

L. A. Nixon

Plate 68 Below On 5th July 1979, No. 45 064 potters along the down slow line at Sharnbrook with an empty cement train.

L. A. Nixon

Plate 69 Above The 'Brush' works dominate this picture of No. 45 107 pulling away from Loughborough with the 12.04 St. Pancras–Derby express on 29th May 1978.

Gavin Morrison

Plate 70 Below No. 45 114, with the 17.16 St. Pancras–Nottingham express, pulls away from Wellingborough on 16th August 1980.

Gavin Morrison

Plate 71 Right Further north, on the Nottingham extension, the imposing frontage of Nottingham station overshadows the 16.00 to St. Pancras as it leaves headed by No. 45 137 *The Bedfordshire and Hertfordshire Regiment (T.A.)* on 5th May 1979.

Gavin Morrison

Plate 72 Below Two for the price of one just north of Leicester station on 29th May 1978, as No. 45 101 heads the 16.00 Sheffield—St. Pancras and meets No. 45 135 leaving with the 15.55 St. Pancras—Derby.

Gavin Morrison

Focus on Derby

Plate 73 Above On a works open day at Derby on 31st August 1963, No. D107 (45 120) leaves with a Newcastle—Bristol express and passes Ivatt Mogul No. 46440 shunting some vans.

T. Boustead

Plate 74 Right No. 45 039 *The Manchester Regiment* passes through the outskirts of Derby as it heads north on a summer Saturday relief from the West of England on 5th August 1978.

Gavin Morrison

Plate 75 Below The platform clock registers 19.26 as No. 45 137 *The Bedfordshire and Hertfordshire Regiment (T.A.)* waits to depart, with a mail train on the evening of 30th January 1980, from platform 4 at Derby.

C. J. Marsden

The Derby—Sheffield Line

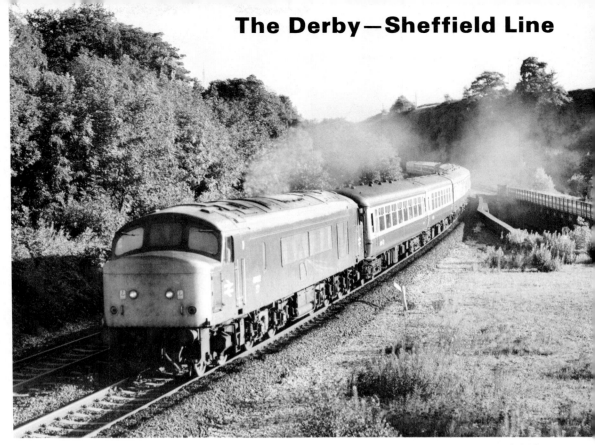

Plate 76 Right On 15th August 1978, Class 46, No. 46 042 glints in the evening sunshine as it rounds the curve at Ambergate on its journey north with a west of England to Newcastle express. The old Midland main line to Manchester, via Peak Forest, can be seen on the right of the picture. This is now singled, terminating at Matlock.

L. A. Nixon

Plate 77 Below   An express from Newcastle hurries south past Duffield headed by No. 46 022 on 29th May 1979.

L. A. Nixon

Plate 82 Left Above On 2nd August 1980, No. 45 062 is ready to depart from Scarborough with the (S.O.) 12.30 to Leicester whilst No. 03 089 shunts empty stock for a later departure.
Gavin Morrison

Plate 83 Left Below On 7th September 1979, an unidentified Class 45 passes this spectacular array of signals at Barrow Hill Junction as it heads a northbound freight.
L. A. Nixon

Plate 84 Right The front ends of the HST and EMU make the design of the Class 46 look very old fashioned. This contrasting line up was taken at King's Cross on 20th March 1980, the 'Peak' being No. 46 031.
John Whiteley

Plate 85 Below On 10th July 1976, before the extensive rationalization of King's Cross, No. 46 038 weaves its way out across the complicated trackwork heading a relief for Newcastle.
Gavin Morrison

The Eastern Region and Kings Cross

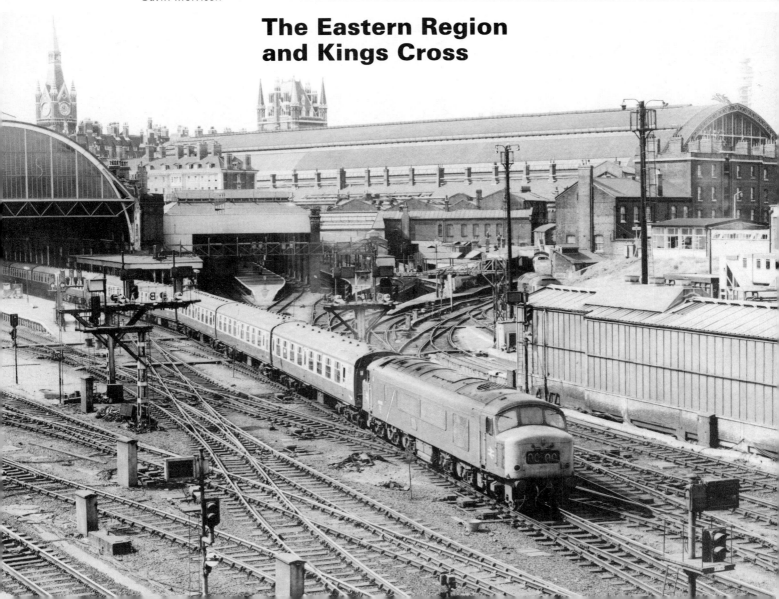

Focus on Bristol

Plate 86 Above Class 45/0, No. D15 (45 018) with a 55A Leeds Holbeck shed plate showing, passes Fishponds as it nears Bristol Temple Meads on 2nd June 1963. The coaling tower of Bristol Barrow Road depot can be seen above the bridge.

John Whiteley

Plate 87 Below No. 45 107, fitted with e.t.h., stands under the overall roof at Bristol Temple Meads as it waits to depart with the 13.56 Penzance—Birmingham on 13th January 1979.

J. Chalcraft

Bristol to Birmingham

Plate 88 Right On 14th August 1978, a very mixed freight from Severn Tunnel Junction passes Croome, in the heart of Worcestershire, headed by No. 45 019.
                                        John Vaughan

Plate 89 Left The low evening sunshine, on 18th August 1978, catches a Class 46 at Wickwar in Gloucestershire whilst working a freightliner train from Cardiff to Newcastle.
                                        John Vaughan

Plate 90 Right An impressive line up of 'Peak' power is seen at Bristol Temple Meads on 29th April 1978. On the left, No. 45 010 waits to depart with the 18.53 to Birmingham, No. 46 049 stands in the centre road with an excursion returning north from Weston-super-Mare and named 'Peak' No. 45 059 *Royal Engineer* stands in platform 3 with a terminating working from Taunton.
                                        J. Chalcraft

Plate 91 Above   The layout of Chinley North Junction is shown in this impressive picture of No. 45 001 taking the Hope Valley Line towards Sheffield, with a Tunstead–Margam train on 15th September 1979.

L. A. Nixon

The Hope Valley Route

Plate 92 Above   A different view of Chinley North Junction, taken on 6th September 1976, showing No. 45 110 heading the 18.06 Manchester to St. Pancras express.

P. J. Robinson

Plate 93 Below   The 18.06 Manchester—St. Pancras is featured again in the delightful Hope Valley countryside. It is seen approaching Hathersage headed by an unidentified 'Peak' in June 1976.

L. A. Nixon

Focus on Manchester

Plate 94 Right On 3rd August 1980, No. 45 032 is seen under the roof of the now closed Manchester Exchange station with a rake of ballast wagons.

Gavin Morrison

Plate 95 Below Two different forms of traction at Manchester Piccadilly on 20th August 1980. No. 45 021 is leaving with the 15.15 to Harwich, whilst a Class 86 electric locomotive prepares to depart for Birmingham New Street.

Gavin Morrison

Plate 96 Above Whitchurch (Salop) signal box towers above No. 46 025 as it passes non-stop heading the 10.00 Crewe—Cardiff train on 22nd September 1979.

Gavin Morrison

Plate 97 Below The pleasant Shropshire countryside is featured in this picture of No. 46 022 at Marshbrook as it heads the (S.O.) 08.45 Newquay—Manchester Piccadilly train on 22nd September 1979.

John Whiteley

The North and West Route

Plate 98 Above A Northfield to York special passes Oakenshaw North Junction near Normanton, West Yorkshire, on 3rd May 1980, headed by No. 45 008.

Gavin Morrison

Plate 99 Below A Sheffield bound refurbished DMU meets 'Peak', No. 46 039, which appears in need of a repaint, as it approaches Rotherham on the 07.30 Birmingham—Newcastle on 21st April 1979. Two Class 08 shunters can be seen working in the yard.

John Whiteley

The Midland between Leeds and Sheffield

Plate 100 Above At Goose Hill Junction, Normanton, on 15th May 1980, No. 45 056 passes with the 16.05 Nottingham to Carlisle train. In the background, on the right, Class 31, No. 31 120 approaches at the head of a weed killing train.
John Whiteley

Plate 101 Right The decaying remains of Normanton station is passed by No. 45 025 on 8th July 1979, whilst working an up empty stock train.
Gavin Morrison

Focus on Leeds

Plate 104 Above   Having reversed at Leeds and changed locomotives, the 09.35 Carlisle—Nottingham heads south past Holbeck stabling point with No. 45 118 *The Royal Artilleryman* at the head on 12th May 1979.

John Whiteley

Plate 105 Below   On 2nd September 1979, No. 45 056 prepares to move the empty stock off the 07.30 from Swansea away from Leeds station to the carriage sidings at Neville Hill.

John Whiteley

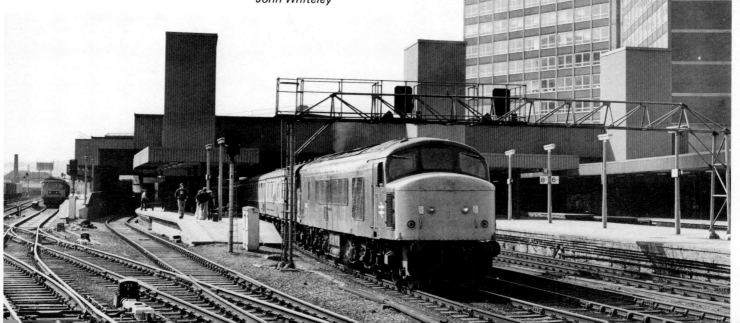

Peaks in West Yorkshire

Plate 106 Left On 15th July 1979, ex-works No. 45 00[...] leaves Bradford Forste[...] Square with empty stock fo[...] Neville Hill, Leeds, afte[...] arriving with an overnigh[...] holiday special from th[...] south. This train had bee[...] diverted from Bradfor[...] Exchange due to enginee[...]ing works. Forster Squar[...] station rarely handles loco[...]motive hauled passenge[...] trains, as most of the loca[...] services are DMU hauled.

Gavin Morriso[...]

Plate 107 Below The paris[...] church at Shipley stands ou[...] clearly on the skyline as th[...] 09.35 Carlisle—Nottingha[...] passes Guiseley Junctio[...] headed by No. 45 066 o[...] 20th October 1979.

John Whiteley

Plate 108 Right The old and the new architecture blend in this view of Bradford showing Laira-allocated Class 46, 'Peak', No. 46 006 as it approaches Laisterdyke on 4th May 1979 with a Rugby League Cup Final Special to King's Cross.
John Whiteley

Plate 109 Below No. 45 015 is seen about to enter Marsh Lane cutting, Leeds on 29th September 1979, at the head of the 12.05 Liverpool to York express.
Gavin Morrison

Plate 110 Left Class 45 No. 45 035, is seen passing through the picturesque woods at Rodley, just before the trees come into full leaf. It is heading the 10.25 Nottingham to Glasgow train on 26th March 1980.

John Whiteley

Plate 111 Below On 22nd July 1976, Class 46, No. 46 034 coasts down the bank from Morley Tunnel with the 07.55 Newcastle to Liverpool train as it approaches Batley, and the parish church dominates the skyline. This was once a very busy junction where the London North Western and Great Northern Railways met. The earthworks which once carried the GN can be seen on the right of the picture.

Gavin Morrison

Plate 112 Above Like so many ex-Lancashire and Yorkshire stations, Halifax is now but a shadow of its former self, and on 12th September 1981 No. 45 003 pulls away from what now remains, with the summer Saturdays only 07.57 Weymouth to Bradford Exchange.

John Whiteley

Plate 113 Below The 14.47 York—Liverpool passes Mirfield on 24th September 1979 headed by No. 45 013 allocated to York. The coat of arms of the City of York can be seen just above the locomotive number.

Gavin Morrison

Plate 114 Left Approaching Standedge Tunnel round the 'S' bend from Marsden on 23rd August 1975, is No. 46 035 heading the 10.02 Newcastle to Liverpool train. The Huddersfield and Ashton Canal boat repair warehouse can be seen on the left of the picture.

Gavin Morrison

Plate 115 Below On 27th September 1979, the 11.05 Liverpool–York rushes down the bank from Marsden to Huddersfield and into the deep cutting at Paddock headed by No. 46 049. The trackbed of the lifted duplicate lines can clearly be seen on the left.

John Whiteley

Peaks in Lancashire

Plate 116 Right Emerging from Liverpool Lime Street cutting with the 11.28 from Newcastle is No. 46 052 on 8th September 1979. 'Deltic' No. 55 018 *Ballymoss*, which had arrived unexpectedly on that day on a train from Newcastle, waits to back on to the stock for the return working.

Gavin Morrison

Plate 117 Left The (S.O.) 13.00 Blackpool—Bradford comes very slowly through the platform at Blackburn headed by No. 45 028 on 18th August 1979.

Gavin Morrison

Plate 118 Below On 9th September 1979, No. 46 046 is seen climbing Miles Platting bank, out of Manchester Victoria, at the head of the Sunday 10.40 Liverpool—Newcastle, which was being diverted via the Calder Valley main line. Red Bank carriage sidings can be seen in the top right of the picture.

John Whiteley

Plate 119 Left With th 08.40 diverted Sunda working from Liverpoo to Newcastle on 16th September 1979, No 46 046 is seen in picturesque section o the Calder Valley be tween Horsfall Tunne and Castle Hill Tunne about two miles east o Todmorden.

John Whiteley

Plate 120 Below On 22nd March 1980, No 45 046 *Royal Fusilier* rushes up the Calder Valley and approaches Hebden Bridge at the head of the diverted 10.25 Nottingham–Glasgow. A failed DMU can be seen in the loop on the right.

Gavin Morrison

Diversions on the Calder Valley Main Line

Plate 121 Above On 9th July 1978, No. 46 045, heading the diverted Sunday 09.25 Newcastle—Liverpool, emerges from Winterbutlee Tunnel, near Walsden, on the climb from Todmorden Summit Tunnel.

Gavin Morrison

Plate 122 Left No. 45 121 passes the site of the long since vanished Border Counties Junction, at Hexham, on 4th June 1978, heading a Wellingborough to Carlisle day excursion. The River Tyne can just be seen above the locomotive.

P. J. Robinson

Plate 123 Centre Having worked through from Leeds on 13th April 1963, No. D159 (46 022), enters Carlisle with the down 'Thames—Clyde Express'.

John Whiteley

Plate 124 Bottom Class 46, No. 46 046 trundles beneath the distinctive N E R signal box at Hexham on 26th September 1976 with a train of spent ballast.

P. J. Robinson

Between Newcastle and Carlisle

In the North East

Plate 125 Right A policeman keeps the unusually large crowd on the platform, at Darlington, as No. 46 030 arrives from the north with empty stock for a returning special for the crowds which attended the 150 year celebration parade, from Shildon to Darlington, on 31st August 1975.

L. A. Nixon

Plate 126 Below In attractive County Durham, No. 46 048 hurries across Relly Mill Viaduct as it approaches Durham City with the 07.30 Birmingham to Newcastle on 30th March 1978.

P. J. Robinson

Plate 127 Above   On 18th July 1979, a very clean No. 46 034 enters the permanent way sidings in the midst of Tyne Yard with a train of new ballast from Belford.

P. J. Robinson

The Main Line North of Newcastle

Plate 128 Left Arriving at Berwick upon Tweed on 17th August 1977 is No. 46 048 with the 09.50 Edinburgh—Plymouth, having overtaken No. 40 198 in the up loop.
Gavin Morrison

Plate 129 Below The skyline of Newcastle stands out clearly in this photograph of No. 45 008 crossing Byker Bridge, as it heads north for Edinburgh with a 'Holiday Preview' excursion from Chesterfield on 5th March 1977.

P. J. Robinson

Plate 130 Right Seen near Houndwood in the picturesque Border Country, descending from Grantshouse towards Berwick upon Tweed, is No. 46 047, working an up Saturday relief train on 29th July 1978.
Gavin Morrison

Plate 131 Below Class 46, No. 46 042, heads the 15.45 Edinburgh to Liverpool, and is seen in superb scenery on 29th July 1978, climbing to the summit at Grantshouse from Cockburnspath, near Penmanshiel Tunnel.
P. J. Robinson

Plate 132 Above Wild Boar Fell dominates this picture of No. 45 052 approaching the summit of the line at Ais Gill with the 11.50 Glasgow—Nottingham.

John Whiteley

Plate 133 Right One of the many stations now closed, on the northern section of the line, is at Culgaith, and No. 45 061 is seen passing some of the former station buildings whilst heading the 11.50 Glasgow to Nottingham on 22nd November 1980. The signal box, however, still survives and controls the level crossing.

John Whiteley

Plate 134 Above Left The rugged moorland scenery which is so much a feature of the highest sections of the Settle and Carlisle line can be seen in this picture of an unidentified 'Peak' crossing Lunds Viaduct, shortly after passing Garsdale, with the Saturday 09.40 Leicester—Glasgow on 30th September 1978.

Gavin Morrison

Plate 135 Below Left On 8th April 1980, a brief ray of sunshine catches No. 46 053 shortly after passing Ais Gill Summit and starting the long descent to Carlisle with the 10.25 Nottingham to Glasgow.

John Whiteley

Plate 137 Below Coasting down the hill towards Settle Junction, at Helwith Bridge, on 8th April 1980, is No. 45 114 heading the 09.35 Carlisle to Nottingham train.

John Whiteley

Plate 136 Above The lovely Eden Valley at Baron Wood, near Armathwaite, is seen in this picture of No. 45 024 heading the Saturday 11.50 Glasgow—Nottingham on 26th April 1980.

John Whiteley

Peaks in Former Glasgow and South Western Territory

Plate 138 Above The 07.15, from Nottingham to Glasgow Central, leaves Kilmarnock on 2nd June 1977, with No. 45 070 in charge.

B. Morrison

Plate 139 Left On 20th July 1964, No. D19 (45 025) is seen crossing the River Ayr and approaching Ayr station with a relief from Glasgow St. Enoch.

D. Cross

Plate 140 Below Left On 1st August 1966, No. D65 (45 111) *Grenadier Guardsman*, heading a car train to Stranraer, is seen near Pinmore, about 4 miles south of Girvan. This line is now singled all the way from Ayr to Stranraer.

D. Cross

Plate 141 Below The 10.35 Leeds to Glasgow, passes Kirkconnel behind No. D18 (45 121) on 30th August 1962.

D. Cross

te 142 Right On
July 1964, No. D70
ds the up 'Thames—
de Express' through
mlanrig gorge, in
beautiful Nith
ley. This locomo-
e was later named
e Royal Marines, and
umbered 45 048. It
pictured working
ween Sanquhar and
ronbridge.

D. Cross

Plate 143 Left On 28th
April 1962, the afternoon
Glasgow—Leeds headed by
No. D11 (45 122) is cross-
ing Templin Viaduct, near
New Cumnock.

D. Cross

late 144 Right No.
015 (45 018) is seen
auling the morning
eeds to Glasgow train
n 4th July 1964 over
arronbridge Viaduct.
his is another of the
tone viaducts, so much
feature of the old
lasgow & South
estern Railway.

D. Cross

Plate 145 Above On Wednesday, 19th December 1979, No. 45 042 passes Llanwern, near Newport, South Wales, with an up 'Railfreight' train with added coal wagons.

John Vaughan

Plate 146 Below Class 45, No. 45 007 passes slowly through Westbury before reversing and heading towards Salisbury with a stone train from Yeoman Fosters on 14th September 1979.

Gavin Morrison

Freight Variations

Plate 147 Above　　On 14th April 1981, No. 45 061 crosses over at Stapleford & Sandiacre before reversing its very mixed freight into Toton yard.

John Whiteley

Plate 148 Below　　On 7th July 1979, No. 46 040 approaches Durham, past the site of Relly Mill Junction, with a down loose-coupled freight.

P. J. Robinson

Livery Changes

Plate 149 Left On 10th May 1962, an afternoon Morecambe to Leeds express leaves Bingley headed by No. D67 (45 118) later named *The Royal Artilleryman.* The locomotive is in the original green livery with the addition of the yellow nose warning panel, which looked very smart, especially at the head of a rake of maroon coaches.

Gavin Morrison

Plate 150 Below No. 45 114 seen leaving Sheffield with th 15.00 service to St. Pancras o Saturday, 15th September 1979 The locomotive had bee specially painted by Toto depot and had a white roof an red buffer beam which certainl helps to brighten up the du standard blue livery.

John Whitele